THE FAMILY SHEPHERD FIELD MANUAL

Based on the book by Eli Williams

A 4-Hour Workshop for 21st Century Fathers

Guiding, Serving, and Protecting Your Family with Courage and Commitment

Participant Name: _____

Date: _____ **Facilitator:** _____

Table of Contents

WELCOME

Thank you for investing in your family today. This workbook is your personal tool for engaging with the material, reflecting on your role as a father, and creating actionable commitments.

How to Use This Workbook:

- Take notes during presentations
- Complete reflection questions honestly
- Participate in activities and discussions
- Record your personal commitments
- Keep this workbook for future reference and accountability

Ground Rules for Today:

- **Confidentiality** - What's shared here stays here
- **Respect** - Honor every father's journey
- **No Judgment** - We're all learning and growing
- **Participation** - Engage at your comfort level
- **Openness** - Be willing to learn and change
- **Other** _____

Prayer

SESSION 1: THE SHEPHERD'S HEART

Understanding Your Role (50 minutes)

Opening Activity: "Why I'm Here"

My name: _____

My children (names and ages):

One hope I have for my relationship with my children:

The "State of the Flock" Audit

Be honest with yourself. Rate your current level of **active presence** in the following areas on a scale of 1–10 (1 = Absent/Passive, 10 = Fully Engaged).

Area of Presence	Rating (1-10)	One reason for this score:
Spiritual (Leading in prayer; reading the bible to/with; teaching values)		
Emotional (Present; knowing their hearts/fears; empathy/intimacy)		
Physical (Being there; play; protection)		
Intellectual (Knowing their school/interests)		

Breakout Discussion Notes:

- In which area are your children "wandering" the most right now?

- What is one obstacle keeping you from being more present?

The Shepherd Metaphor

Key Characteristics of the Ancient Shepherd:

1. **Constant Presence** - The shepherd was with the flock 24/7
2. **Intimate Knowledge** - He knew each sheep by name and temperament
3. **Active Protection** - He fought off predators with rod and staff
4. **Provision** - He led them to food, water, and safe rest
5. **Sacrifice** - He put the flock's needs above his own comfort

Scripture Foundation:

"The Lord is my shepherd; I shall not want." - Psalm 23 *(Recite together)*

"Children are a heritage from the Lord, offspring a reward from him." - Psalm 127:3

The Modern Application - My children need a shepherd who is:

- **Present** (not just physically, but emotionally engaged)
- **Protective** (guarding against modern dangers)
- **Providing** (more than just financially)
- **Patient** (understanding their developmental needs)
- **Purposeful** (leading with intention, not just reacting)

Personal Reflection:

Which of these five characteristics is my greatest strength as a father?

Which one do I most need to develop?

"The shepherd doesn't just own or manage the sheep; he knows them."

The Crisis and the Call

The Fatherlessness Epidemic - Key Statistics:

- Nearly 1 in 4 children in America grow up without a father in the home
- Children without engaged fathers face significantly higher risks
- 78% of Christian fathers do not regularly read or discuss scripture with their children
- 83% of Christian fathers do not pray with them outside of mealtimes or bedtimes
- Only 26% of Christian fathers report spending time helping their children grow in Bible knowledge and spiritual maturity

The Two Types of Shepherds (John 10:12-13):

1. **The Hired Hand** - Works for wages, flees when danger comes, cares more about himself than the flock
2. **The Owner/Family Shepherd** - Has personal investment, stays during crisis, knows each sheep intimately, willing to sacrifice

Honest Self-Assessment:

Which type of shepherd does my daily behavior reflect right now? (Circle one)

Mostly Hired Hand ←——————————————→ Mostly Family Shepherd

1———2———3———4———5———6———7———8———9———10

What specific behaviors led me to this rating?

The Shepherd's Tools and Presence

The Ancient Shepherd's Weapons:

- **The Rod** - A heavy club for fighting predators (protection/defense)
- **The Staff** - A long crook for guiding and rescuing sheep (guidance/correction)
- **The Sling** - For long-range defense and gentle course correction

"Even though I walk through the darkest valley, I will fear no evil, for you are with me; your rod and your staff, they comfort me." - Psalm 23:4

Modern Translation:

- **Your Rod** = The firm boundaries and non-negotiables you establish
- **Your Staff** = The gentle guidance and correction you provide
- **Your Sling** = The proactive teaching and preventive measures you take

My Current "Weapons":

My Rod (one firm boundary I maintain well):

My Staff (one way I guide my children effectively):

My Sling (one proactive measure I take):

The Truth About Time

The Dangerous Myth: "Quality time is more important than quantity."

The Truth: Your children need BOTH.

Common Distractions That Steal My Presence:

Check all that apply to you:

☐ Smartphones/social media
☐ Excessive work hours
☐ Sports fanaticism
☐ Gaming
☐ Substance use
☐ Television/streaming
☐ Hobbies that exclude family
☐ Other: _____

The Cost of Distraction:

- Weakened emotional bonds
- Difficulty with emotional regulation in children
- Low self-worth
- Missed opportunities for influence
- Loss of trust

Personal Reflection:

What is my biggest distraction from being fully present with my children?

How many hours per week does this distraction consume?

Session 1 Closing Activity: Personal Commitment

1. One specific "predator" (distraction) I will protect my family from this week:

2. One way I will increase my fully-present time with my children:

3. One person I will share this commitment with for accountability:

Name: _____

Contact: _____

When I'll share: _____

Session 1 Notes & Reflections

Use this space for additional thoughts, questions, or insights:

SESSION 2: LEADING THROUGH THE VALLEYS

Protecting Your Family from Modern Dangers (50 minutes)

Opening: The Reality of the Valley

"Even though I walk through the darkest valley, I will fear no evil, for you are with me." - Psalm 23:4

Your role as shepherd in the valley:

- Be present
- Use your tools
- Maintain vision
- Model courage
- Other _____

> *"A shepherd doesn't wait for the wolf to strike; he anticipates the attack."*

Wolf (predator) Identification

List the top 3 "modern wolves" threatening your family's peace or safety today:

1. _____

2. _____

3. _____

Tools: The Staff, Rod & Sling Strategy

- **The Staff (Guidance/Comfort):** How can I draw my child closer to me this week?

  - *Action:* _____

- **The Rod (Correction/Protection):** What boundary do I need to reinforce or build?

  - *Action:* _____

- **The Sling (Prevention):** What intentional, advance measures do I need to take?
  - *Action:* _____

The Scope of the Problem:

- Global adult entertainment market: $58-66 billion (projected to reach $93-100 billion by early 2030s)
- Average age of first exposure: 12-13 years old
- Children encounter pornography on social media as often as on adult websites

The Grave Hazards:

- Distorted views of sexuality and relationships
- Confusion and emotional distress
- Increased vulnerability to exploitation
- Normalization of unhealthy behaviors
- Premature sexualization
- Impact on brain development

Scripture Foundation:

"I will set nothing wicked before my eyes..." – Psalm 101:3

Personal Assessment:

Have I had age-appropriate conversations with my children about pornography?

☐ Yes, comprehensive conversations
☐ Yes, but only briefly
☐ No, not yet
☐ Not applicable (children too young)

If no or only briefly, what has prevented me from having this conversation?

Age-Appropriate Guidance Framework

Early Childhood (Preschool/Elementary):

- Focus: Body safety and boundaries
- Key topics: Private parts, appropriate touch, respect for bodies

Middle Childhood (Pre-Teens):

- Focus: Puberty, curiosity, and accidental exposure
- Key topics: Body changes, device safety, healthy relationships

Adolescence (Teens):

- Focus: Risks, consequences, and self-esteem
- Key topics: Impact on relationships, accurate sexuality information, consent and respect

My Action Plan:

For each of my children, what conversation do I need to have next?

Child's name: _____ Age: _____ Next conversation topic:

Child's name: _____ Age: _____ Next conversation topic:

Child's name: _____ Age: _____ Next conversation topic:

Practical Protection Tips

1. Create a Safe Environment - Be the trusted, non-judgmental guide

2. Choose the Right Time - Relaxed, distraction-free moments

3. Listen Actively - Validate feelings, don't just lecture

4. Set Clear Boundaries - Especially for technology use

5. Monitor Appropriately - You're responsible for the safety of minors

My Current Technology Boundaries:

What rules do I currently have for my children's device use?

What additional boundaries do I need to establish?

When a Child Has Been Exposed: The Six-Step Rescue Plan

1. Stay Calm - Resist panic and anger

2. Initiate Conversation - Express love and concern, not disappointment

3. Provide Education - Discuss unrealistic portrayals and potential harm

4. Set Boundaries - Clear rules and safeguards for devices

5. Seek Professional Help - If needed, don't hesitate

6. Ongoing Support - This is a long-term commitment

If I discover my child has been exposed, my first three actions will be:

1. _____

2. _____

3. _____

The Dark Valley Part 2: Other Modern Dangers

1. Youth Gambling - The New Normal

The Trends:

- 60-80% of high school students have gambled in the past year
- Youth problem gambling rates (4-8%) are DOUBLE adult rates (~1%)
- Online sports betting normalized through constant advertising
- "Loot boxes" in video games directly linked to gambling problems

Why This Matters:

- Teenage brain's decision-making center isn't fully developed until mid-20s
- Problem gambling linked to depression, anxiety, substance abuse
- Gambling addiction has one of the highest suicide rates among all addictions

"Dishonest money dwindles away, but whoever gathers money little by little makes it grow."
- Proverbs 13:11

My Action Steps:

Have I talked to my children about gambling risks? ☐ Yes ☐ No

Do my children play games with loot boxes or in-game purchases? ☐ Yes ☐ No ☐ Don't know

Do I model healthy behavior around gambling? ☐ Yes ☐ No ☐ Need to improve

One conversation I need to have about gambling:

2. Self-Harm and Mental Health

Warning Signs to Watch For:

☐ Unexplained cuts, bruises, or burns
☐ Wearing long sleeves/pants in warm weather
☐ Withdrawal from activities
☐ Expressions of hopelessness or worthlessness
☐ Changes in eating or sleeping patterns

Crisis Resources (Write these in your phone NOW):

- National Suicide & Crisis Lifeline: **988**
- Crisis Text Line: Text **HOME** to **741741**

"The Lord is close to the brokenhearted and saves those who are crushed in spirit." - Psalm 34:18

Personal Reflection:

How would I rate my awareness of my children's mental and emotional state?

Low Awareness ←————————————————→ **High Awareness**

1———2———3———4———5———6———7———8———9———10

What can I do to increase my awareness?

3. Entertainment Hazards

Five Keys to Wholesome Choices:

1. **Align with Your Values** - What are your family's non-negotiables?
2. **Consider Age-Appropriateness** - Pay attention to ratings
3. **Seek Positive Themes** - Look for content that reinforces virtues
4. **Encourage Critical Thinking** - Discuss characters' choices
5. **Prioritize Quality Over Popularity** - Don't be swayed by hype

"Finally, brothers and sisters, whatever is true, whatever is noble, whatever is right, whatever is pure, whatever is lovely, whatever is admirable—if anything is excellent or praiseworthy—think about such things." - Philippians 4:8

My Family's Entertainment Values:

Our non-negotiables (content we will not allow):

How I will enforce these standards:

Interactive Activity: "Protecting the Fold" - Scenario Workshop

Work with a partner on these real-world scenarios:

Scenario 1: You discover your 13-year-old has been viewing pornography on their phone. What do you do in the next 24 hours?

My response plan:

Scenario 2: Your 10-year-old comes home talking about a new video game all their friends are playing. It's rated M for Mature (17+). How do you handle it?

My response plan:

Scenario 3: You notice your 15-year-old has become withdrawn, is wearing long sleeves constantly, and their grades are dropping. What's your first move?

My response plan:

Key insights from partner discussion:

Session 2 Closing: The Shepherd's Vigilance

"Be strong and courageous. Do not be afraid; do not be discouraged, for the Lord your God will be with you wherever you go." - Joshua 1:9

Personal Commitment:

1. The one "valley" (danger) my family is most vulnerable to right now:

2. One specific protective action I'll take this week:

Session 2 Notes & Reflections

SESSION 3: THE SHEPHERD AS SERVANT LEADER

Guiding with Humility (50 minutes)

Opening Activity: "Leadership Styles" Quick Assessment

Rate yourself honestly on a scale of 1-10:

I prioritize my children's needs over my personal comfort

Rarely ←————————————————→ **Consistently**

1————2————3————4————5————6————7————8————9————10

I apologize to my children when I make mistakes

Rarely ←————————————————→ **Consistently**

1————2————3————4————5————6————7————8————9————10

I model the behavior I expect from my children

Rarely ←————————————————→ **Consistently**

1————2————3————4————5————6————7————8————9————10

What does my assessment reveal about my leadership style?

The Servant Leader Model

"True authority is found in the depth of your service."

The Powerful Example:

In John 13:3-5, Jesus washed his disciples' feet—the job of the lowest servant.

"For even the Son of Man did not come to be served, but to serve, and to give his life as a ransom for many." - Mark 10:45

Key Characteristics of the Servant Shepherd:

1. **Emphasis on Service** - Sees role as serving family, not ruling over them
2. **Empathy** - Can put himself in his children's shoes
3. **Listening** - Makes time to truly hear his family
4. **Humility** - Doesn't see himself as above mundane tasks
5. **Empowerment** - Helps family members make age-appropriate decisions

The Contrast:

Authoritarian Father	Servant Leader Father
"Do it because I said so"	"Let me explain why this matters"
Rarely explains reasoning	Provides age-appropriate reasoning
Sees questioning as disrespect	Welcomes questions and dialogue
Mistakes are never admitted	Apologizes when wrong
Children obey out of fear	Children follow out of trust and respect

Personal Reflection:

Which column more accurately describes my current approach?

What is one specific way I can shift toward servant leadership this week?

1. Empathy and Understanding

Example Scenario: Your 8-year-old is melting down about homework.

Authoritarian response: "Stop crying and do your work!"

Servant leader response: "This seems really frustrating. Tell me what's making this hard."

My Practice:

Think of a recent situation where my child was struggling. How did I respond?

How could I have responded with more empathy?

The "Wash the Feet" Assessment

What is the heaviest burden my wife or children are carrying right now? (Financial stress, school anxiety, loneliness, etc.)

- **The Burden:** _____

My Service Commitment

I, _____, commit to taking over the following task/chore this week to lighten the load of my family:

- **The Task:** _____

- **When I will do it:** _____

2. Empowerment and Autonomy

Example Scenario: Your 12-year-old wants to organize their own birthday party.

Authoritarian response: "I'll handle it. You're too young."

Servant leader response: "Great idea! Let's make a plan together. What's your budget?"

My Practice:

What is one age-appropriate responsibility I can delegate to each of my children?

Child: _____ Responsibility: _____

Child: _____ Responsibility: _____

Child: _____ Responsibility: _____

Example Scenario: You lose your temper and yell at your child unfairly.

Authoritarian response: Justifies behavior, blames child

Servant leader response: "I was wrong to yell at you like that. I was stressed about work, but that's not your fault. I'm sorry. Will you forgive me?"

"Fathers, do not embitter your children, or they will become discouraged." - Colossians 3:21

My Practice:

Is there a situation where I need to apologize to one of my children?

☐ Yes ☐ No

If yes, what will I say?

When will I do this? _____

Loving and Serving Your Partner

"Husbands, love your wives, just as Christ loved the church and gave himself up for her." - Ephesians 5:25

Servant Leadership in Marriage:

- Give full attention when she speaks
- Be an equal partner in chores and childcare
- Support her personal and professional goals
- Apologize sincerely when you make mistakes

The Challenge: Try to "out-serve" your partner this week.

Three specific ways I will serve my partner this week:

Discipline That Nurtures

The True Meaning of Discipline: Discipline is not punishment—it's teaching and training.

"Start children off on the way they should go, and even when they are old they will not turn from it." - Proverbs 22:6

The Five Keys to Guiding Your Flock:

1. Clear Fences and Pastures (Set Clear Expectations)

What are three clear, consistent rules in my household?

2. Treats and Rest (Provide Positive Reinforcement)

How do I currently praise and reward my children's good behavior?

3. Feeling the Thistle (Use Natural Consequences)

What is one area where I can allow my children to experience safe, natural consequences?

4. The Gentle Staff (Avoid Physical Punishment)

"Fathers, do not exasperate your children; instead, bring them up in the training and instruction of the Lord." - Ephesians 6:4

Do I currently use physical punishment? ☐ Yes ☐ No ☐ Sometimes

What alternative discipline methods can I use instead?

5. Modeling the Path (Guidance and Support)

What behavior do I expect from my children that I need to model better myself?

The Foundation: Love

"Love is patient, love is kind... It always protects, always trusts, always hopes, always perseveres." - 1 Corinthians 13:4-7

Personal Reflection:

How well do I communicate unconditional love to each of my children?

Child: _____ How I show love: _____

Child: _____ How I show love: _____

Child: _____ How I show love: _____

What is one additional way I can express love to each child this week?

Session 3 Closing: The Servant Leader's Promise

Servant leadership is not weakness—it's the strongest form of leadership because it's rooted in love, not fear.

Personal Commitment:

1. One area where I need to shift from "scepter" to "towel" (from authoritarian to servant):

2. One specific act of humble service I'll perform for my family this week:

Session 3 Notes & Reflections

SESSION 4: SHEPHERDING UNDER STRESS

"A panicked shepherd makes for a scattered flock."

Managing Pressure and Prioritizing Presence (50 minutes)

Opening: "Stress Check-In"

My current stress level:

Low Stress ←————————————————→ **Extremely High Stress**

1———2———3———4———5———6———7———8———9———10

My top two stressors (check all that apply):

☐ Work/financial pressure
☐ Time demands
☐ Relationship challenges
☐ Children's behavioral issues
☐ Health concerns
☐ Other: _____

The Reality of Parental Stress

The Statistics:

- 33% of parents report high stress levels (vs. 20% of non-parents)
- 48% of parents report feeling completely overwhelmed most days
- 41% of parents report being so stressed they cannot function

Common Pressures on Fathers:

- Financial strain
- Time demands
- Exhaustion
- Behavioral challenges
- Societal pressure
- Isolation
- Inner turmoil

The Truth: An overwhelmed, burned-out father cannot effectively shepherd his family. Your well-being is not selfish—it's foundational.

"Come to me, all you who are weary and burdened, and I will give you rest." - Matthew 11:28-30

Strategies for the Resilient Shepherd

1. Sharpen Your Tools: Prioritize Self-Care

The Oxygen Mask Principle: Put on your oxygen mask first before helping your child.

Practical Steps:

☐ **Schedule "Me Time"** - 10-15 minutes daily, non-negotiable

☐ **Prioritize Sleep** - 7-9 hours nightly

☐ **Nourish and Move** - Balanced meals, regular exercise

☐ **Practice Mindfulness** - Deep breathing, meditation, prayer, or simple quiet time

My Self-Care Action Plan:

One self-care practice I will start this week:

When I will do it (specific time): _____

How I will protect this time: _____

2. Build Your Support Flank

No shepherd should work alone.

"Two are better than one, because they have a good return for their labor: If either of them falls down, one can help the other up." - Ecclesiastes 4:9-10

Practical Steps:

☐ **Connect with Fellow Fathers** - Share experiences

☐ **Lean on Family and Friends** - Ask for help

☐ **Tend Your Marriage** - Communicate openly

☐ **Join a Support Group** - Find or create a community

☐ **Seek God's Strength** - Prayer and faith provide supernatural support

My Support Network:

Three people I can call when I'm struggling:

1. Name: _____ Contact: _____

2. Name: _____ Contact: _____

3. Name: _____ Contact: _____

One way I will strengthen my support network this month:

3. Set Realistic Expectations

You cannot shepherd a perfect flock because perfect flocks don't exist.

Practical Steps:

☐ **Focus on Core Needs** - Prioritize well-being over "ideal" lifestyle

☐ **Practice Self-Compassion** - Treat yourself with kindness

☐ **Let Go of Comparison** - Your family's journey is unique

☐ **Celebrate Small Wins** - Acknowledge daily victories

My Realistic Expectations:

One unrealistic expectation I need to release:

Three small wins I can celebrate from this past week:

1. _____

2. _____

3. _____

4. Establish Order and Boundaries

Routines reduce chaos; boundaries protect your energy.

Practical Steps:

☐ **Consistent Routines** - Regular bedtimes, mealtimes

☐ **Healthy Boundaries** - Say "no" to overextending

☐ **Protect Family Time** - Guard evenings and weekends

☐ **Limit Technology** - Set device-free times and spaces

My Boundaries and Routines:

One routine I will establish or strengthen:

One boundary I need to set (at work, with extended family, etc.):

Our family's device-free times will be:

5. Seek Wisdom and Professional Counsel

Important Note for Men: The strongest men are those who recognize when they need support and have the courage to ask for it.

"Where there is no guidance, a people falls, but in an abundance of counselors there is safety." - Proverbs 11:14

Do I need professional help for:

☐ Stress management
☐ Anger issues
☐ Depression or anxiety
☐ Marriage counseling
☐ Parenting guidance
☐ Substance use
☐ Other: _____

If I checked any boxes above, I will:

☐ Research counselors/therapists this week
☐ Ask my doctor for a referral
☐ Call my insurance for covered providers
☐ Reach out to my faith community for resources
☐ Contact: _____

The "Driveway Ritual"

To prevent the stress of the world from entering my home, I will practice this 2-minute "re-entry" habit before I walk through the front door:

- **Step 1 (Physical):** (e.g., Leave the phone in the console, take 5 deep breaths)

- **Step 2 (Mental/Spiritual):** (e.g., A 30-second prayer: *"Lord, help me leave work here and give my best to my flock."*)

The Power of Rest

Working from Rest vs. Working from Exhaustion:

Working from Rest	Working from Exhaustion
Enhanced focus	Poor decision-making
Improved creativity	Reduced patience
Greater resilience	Emotional unavailability
Stronger motivation	Increased conflict
Sustainable pace	Risk of burnout

The Importance of Sleep:

Sleep Recommendations:

- Most adults need 7-9 hours nightly
- Consistency is key (same bedtime/wake time daily)

My Current Sleep Pattern:

Average hours per night: _____

Bedtime: _____ Wake time: _____

Quick Tips for Better Sleep:

☐ Stick to consistent sleep schedule
☐ Create dark, cool (65-68°F), quiet environment
☐ Avoid caffeine 4-6 hours before bed
☐ Avoid screens at least 1 hour before bed
☐ Exercise regularly (but not right before bed)

My Sleep Improvement Plan:

One change I will make to improve my sleep:

Starting date: _____

Weekly Rest

"Remember the Sabbath day by keeping it holy." - Exodus 20:8-10

Even Jesus modeled rest: *"Come with me by yourselves to a quiet place and get some rest."* - Mark 6:31

My Day of Rest:

Which day will be my weekly day of rest? _____

What will I do (or not do) on this day?

What obstacles might prevent this, and how will I overcome them?

The Shepherd's Time

The Dangerous Myth: "Quality time is more important than quantity."

The Truth: Your children need BOTH quantity and quality time.

Action Steps for Prioritizing Time:

1. **Schedule It** - Block time in calendar, treat as non-negotiable
2. **Be Present** - Put away phone and distractions
3. **Make It Two-Way** - Ask children what they want to do
4. **Be Consistent** - Even 30 minutes daily makes a difference
5. **Cherish Every Moment** - Your kids don't need perfection; they need presence

My Time Commitment:

How much fully-present time do I currently spend with each child per day?

Child: _____ Current time: _____ minutes/hours

Child: _____ Current time: _____ minutes/hours

Child: _____ Current time: _____ minutes/hours

How much time do I want to spend with each child per day?

Child: _____ Goal time: _____ minutes/hours

Child: _____ Goal time: _____ minutes/hours

Child: _____ Goal time: _____ minutes/hours

When will this time happen each day?

What will I do to protect this time?

Session 4 Closing Activity: "The Shepherd's Covenant"

I commit to:

1. Protecting my family from:

2. Being fully present by:

3. Leading with humility through:

4. Managing my stress by:

5. Prioritizing rest by:

I will share this commitment with:

Name: _____

Contact: _____

When: _____

I will check my progress on: _____

"The flock is only as healthy as the shepherd."

Session 4 Notes & Reflections

WORKSHOP CONCLUSION

The Shepherd's Legacy

What You've Learned Today:

1. Your role as shepherd is essential—your presence matters
2. Modern dangers require active, informed protection
3. True leadership is service, not dominance
4. Your well-being is foundational to your family's security
5. Both quantity and quality time are necessary
6. God's wisdom and strength are available to guide you

The Ripple Effect:

When you become a better father:

- Your children thrive
- Your family strengthens
- Your community improves
- Future generations benefit

Strong fathers build strong families.
Strong families build strong communities.
Strong communities build a better world.

The Challenge

You cannot be a perfect father—no one can. But you can be:

- **Present**
- **Protective**
- **Purposeful**
- **Patient**
- **Persistent**

Your children don't need a perfect shepherd. They need YOU—fully present, courageously committed, and humbly serving.

"These commandments that I give you today are to be on your hearts. Impress them on your children. Talk about them when you sit at home and when you walk along the road, when you lie down and when you get up." - Deuteronomy 6:6-7

Final Activity: "One Thing"

The one thing I'm taking from today is:

My 30-Day Action Plan

Week 1 (Days 1-7):

Primary focus: _____

Specific actions:

Week 2 (Days 8-14):

Primary focus: _____

Specific actions:

Week 3 (Days 15-21):

Primary focus: _____

Specific actions:

Week 4 (Days 22-30):

Primary focus: _____

Specific actions:

Accountability Check-In Schedule

I will review my progress:

☐ Weekly on: _____

☐ Bi-weekly on: _____

☐ Monthly on: _____

I will check in with my accountability partner:

☐ Weekly
☐ Bi-weekly
☐ Monthly

Method: ☐ Phone call ☐ Text ☐ In-person ☐ Video call

Resources and Next Steps

Recommended Reading

☐ *The Family Shepherd: Guiding, Serving and Protecting Your Family with Love, Courage, and Enduring Faith* by Eli Williams (full book for deeper study)

☐ *Fathering Strong: God's Blueprint for Leading Your Family* by Bruce Stapleton

☐ *Father Love: The Powerful Resource Every Child Needs* by Eli Williams (updated and revised)

☐ *Good Pictures Bad Pictures: Porn-Proofing Today's Young Kids* by Kristen Jenson

☐ *The Whole-Brain Child* by Daniel J. Siegel and Tina Payne Bryson

☐ *How to Talk So Kids Will Listen & Listen So Kids Will Talk* by Adele Faber and Elaine Mazlish

Books I plan to read:

Online Resources

- **Urban Light Ministries:** (Fathering Strong resources) **urbanlight.org**
- **Fathering Strong© mobile app*:** (for building virtual fatherhood communities) **fatheringstrong.com**
- **National Fatherhood Initiative:** (provider of fatherhood resources and training) **fatherhood.org**
- **Dad.info:** (free expert advice and support for fathers) **dad.info**
- **National Responsible Fatherhood Clearinghouse:** (fatherhood-focused resources for dads and practitioners) **fatherhood.gov**

Crisis Resources

SAVE THESE IN YOUR PHONE NOW:

- **National Suicide & Crisis Lifeline:** 988
- **Crisis Text Line:** Text HOME to 741741
- **National Problem Gambling Helpline:** 1-800-522-4700
- **National Domestic Violence Hotline:** 1-800-799-7233

Local Resources

Facilitator or Workshop Host will provide:

- Local fatherhood programs
- Counseling services
- Support groups
- Community resources

To join the Fathering Strong© virtual community set up for your group, scan the QR Code on the slide on the screen.

Workshop Evaluation

Please take a few minutes to complete the evaluation on pages 45 and 46 to tell us how we did, and how we can improve.

Thank you.

Scripture References

The following Scripture passages were referenced throughout this workshop:

- **Psalm 23:1** - "The Lord is my shepherd; I shall not want" (KJV)
- **Psalm 127:3** - "Children are a heritage from the Lord, offspring a reward from him" (NIV)
- **John 10:12-13** - The hired hand vs. the true shepherd
- **Psalm 23:4** - "Even though I walk through the darkest valley, I will fear no evil, for you are with me; your rod and your staff, they comfort me" (NIV)
- **Psalm 101:3** – "I will set nothing wicked before my eyes" (NKJV)
- **Proverbs 13:11** - "Dishonest money dwindles away, but whoever gathers money little by little makes it grow" (NIV)
- **Psalm 34:18** - "The Lord is close to the brokenhearted and saves those who are crushed in spirit" (NIV)
- **Philippians 4:8** - "Whatever is true, whatever is noble, whatever is right, whatever is pure, whatever is lovely, whatever is admirable—if anything is excellent or praiseworthy—think about such things" (NIV)
- **Joshua 1:9** - "Be strong and courageous. Do not be afraid; do not be discouraged, for the Lord your God will be with you wherever you go" (NIV)
- **John 13:3-5** - Jesus washing the disciples' feet
- **Mark 10:45** - "For even the Son of Man did not come to be served, but to serve, and to give his life as a ransom for many" (NIV)
- **Colossians 3:21** - "Fathers, do not embitter your children, or they will become discouraged"(NIV)
- **Ephesians 5:25** - "Husbands, love your wives, just as Christ loved the church and gave himself up for her"(NIV)
- **Proverbs 22:6** - "Start children off on the way they should go, and even when they are old they will not turn from it"(NIV)
- **Ephesians 6:4** - "Fathers, do not exasperate your children; instead, bring them up in the training and instruction of the Lord" (NIV)
- **1 Corinthians 13:4-7** - The nature of love
- **Matthew 11:28-30** - "Come to me, all you who are weary and burdened, and I will give you rest" (NIV)
- **Ecclesiastes 4:9-10** - "Two are better than one"(NIV)
- **Proverbs 11:14** - "Where there is no guidance, a people falls, but in an abundance of counselors there is safety"(RSV)
- **Exodus 20:8-10** - Remember the Sabbath day
- **Mark 6:31** - Jesus invites his disciples to rest
- **Deuteronomy 6:6-7** - Impressing God's commandments on your children

- **Isaiah 40:11** - "He tends his flock like a shepherd: He gathers the lambs in his arms and carries them close to his heart; he gently leads those that have young" (NIV)

PERSONAL REFLECTION JOURNAL

Use these pages for ongoing reflection after the workshop:

Week 1 Reflections

Date: _____

What went well this week:

Challenges I faced:

How I responded to challenges:

What I learned about myself:

What I learned about my children:

Adjustments I need to make:

Week 2 Reflections

Date: _____

What went well this week:

Challenges I faced:

How I responded to challenges:

What I learned about myself:

What I learned about my children:

Adjustments I need to make:

Week 3 Reflections

Date: _____

What went well this week:

Challenges I faced:

How I responded to challenges:

What I learned about myself:

What I learned about my children:

Adjustments I need to make:

Week 4 Reflections

Date: _____

What went well this week:

Challenges I faced:

How I responded to challenges:

What I learned about myself:

What I learned about my children:

Adjustments I need to make:

30-Day Review

Date: _____

Overall progress assessment:

Low Progress ←——————————————————→ **Excellent Progress**

1———2———3———4———5———6———7———8———9———10

My biggest win from the past 30 days:

My biggest challenge from the past 30 days:

How my relationship with my children has changed:

How I have changed as a father:

My goals for the next 30 days:

Additional Notes

Use these pages for any additional thoughts, prayers, or reflections:

CLOSING CEREMONY

"He tends his flock like a shepherd: He gathers the lambs in his arms and carries them close to his heart; he gently leads those that have young." - Isaiah 40:11

The Final Reflection

The Commissioning

The Charge

The Closing Prayer

THE FAMILY SHEPHERD WORKSHOP

Guiding, Serving, and Protecting Your Family with Courage and Commitment

For more information and resources, visit:

urbanlight.org

fatheringstrong.com

pastoreli.com

THE SHEPHERD'S CREED

I am not a manager; I am a SHEPHERD.

I do not merely own or <u>steward</u> my home; I know the hearts within it.

I renounce the <u>way</u> of the <u>hireling</u>; I will not flee when the valley grows dark.

I will be PRESENT.

Because my flock is only as healthy as the time I invest.

I will lay down my distractions to pick up my children.

I will be PROTECTIVE.

I will carry the Rod of boundaries and the Sling of prevention.

I will not wait for the wolf to strike; I will guard the gates of my home.

I will be a SERVANT.

I lead best when I am kneeling.

I will use my strength to carry the heaviest burdens, not to crush the weak.

I will be PERSISTENT.

I am not a perfect man, but I serve a Perfect Shepherd.

When I stumble, I will rise. When I wander, I will return.

THESE ARE MY SHEEP. THIS IS MY POST. I WILL NOT ABANDON THEM.

Workshop Evaluation

(Complete and Give to the Workshop Facilitator)

Your feedback helps us improve for future workshops.

Date: _____ **Facilitator:** _____

1. Overall Impact

Please rate the following on a scale of 1–5 (1 = Poor, 5 = Excellent):

- **Relevance of content to your life:** 1 2 3 4 5
- **Clarity of the Shepherd Metaphor:** 1 2 3 4 5
- **Quality of the Field Manual/Materials:** 1 2 3 4 5
- **Facilitator's knowledge and delivery:** 1 2 3 4 5

2. Session Breakdown

Which session was most impactful for you? (Circle one)

- **Session 1:** The Shepherd's Heart (Role/Presence)
- **Session 2:** Leading Through Valleys (Modern Dangers/Pornography)
- **Session 3:** The Servant Leader (Humility/Discipline)
- **Session 4:** Shepherding Under Stress (Self-Care/Time)

Why was this session the most impactful?

3. Personal Growth

- **What is the "One Thing" you are most committed to changing in the next 30 days?**

- **Do you feel better equipped to protect your children from modern dangers?**
  ☐ Yes ☐ No ☐ Somewhat
- **How likely are you to recommend this workshop to another father?**
- (Not Likely) 1 2 3 4 5 6 7 8 9 10 (Very Likely)

4. Open Feedback

- **What was the most challenging part of the workshop for you?**

- **What topics do you wish we had spent more time on?**

- **Any additional comments for the facilitator?**

Ongoing Support Options

I am interested in (check all that apply):

☐ Follow-up weekly fatherhood class
☐ Ongoing support group
☐ Follow-up one-day fatherhood workshop
☐ One-on-one coaching
☐ Online fatherhood community
☐ Monthly meetups

My contact information (optional):

Name: _____

Email: _____

Phone: _____

Please provide this evaluation to your facilitator or mail it to: Urban Light Ministries, PO Box 3132 Springfield, OH 45501

--Thank You-

www.ingramcontent.com/pod-product-compliance
Lightning Source LLC
Chambersburg PA
CBHW081540120626

46550CB00009B/2810